cl

Our Changing World

THE TIMELINE LIBRARY

THE HISTORY OF THE LIBRARY

BY BARBARA A. SOMERVILL

◀ 3000 B.C.
Sumerians develop libraries to house clay tablets; Egyptians create libraries to store papyrus scrolls.

▼ 1800
The Library of Congress is founded.

◀ A.D. mid-1400s
Johannes Gutenberg develops movable-type printing.

5000 B.C.	4000	3000	2000	1000	A.D. 0	1000	2000

Content Adviser: Dr. Hermina G.B. Anghelescu, Assistant Professor at the Library and Information Science Program, Wayne State University, Detroit, Michigan

THE CHILD'S WORLD® • CHANHASSEN, MINNESOTA

The Child's World

Published in the United States of America by The Child's World®
PO Box 326 • Chanhassen, MN 55317-0326 • 800-599-READ • www.childsworld.com

ACKNOWLEDGMENTS
The Child's World®: Mary Berendes, Publishing Director

Editorial Directions, Inc.: E. Russell Primm, Editorial Director; Katie Marsico, Managing Editor and Line Editor; Judith Shiffer, Assistant Editor; Rory Mabin and Caroline Wood, Editorial Assistants; Susan Hindman, Copy Editor; Jennifer Martin, Proofreader; Judith Frisbee, Peter Garnham, Olivia Nellums, Chris Simms, and Stephen Carl Wender, Fact Checkers; Tim Griffin/IndexServ, Indexer; Cian Loughlin O'Day, Photo Researcher; Linda S. Koutris, Photo Selector

The Design Lab: Kathleen Petelinsek, Design and Art Production

PHOTOS
Cover/frontispiece: left—Bettmann/Corbis; center—Stefano Bianchetti/Corbis; right—Adam Woolfitt/Corbis.

Interior: 5—LWA/Dann Tardiff/Corbis; 7, 10, 16, 22—The Granger Collection; 9—Archivo Iconografico, S.A./Corbis; 11, 12, 21—Bettmann/Corbis; 13—Vanni Archive/Corbis; 17—Underwood & Underwood/Corbis; 19—William Manning/Corbis; 20—Library of Congress; 25—kolvenback/Alamy Images; 26—Charles O'Rear/Corbis; 29—Shannon Fagan/Stone+/Getty Images.

LIBRARY OF CONGRESS CATALOGING-IN-PUBLICATION DATA
Somervill, Barbara A.
  The history of the library / by Barbara A. Somervill.
     p. cm. — (Our changing world—the timeline library)
  Includes bibliographical references and index.
  ISBN 1-59296-438-9 (lib. bdg. : alk. paper)
  1. Libraries—History—Juvenile literature. I. Title. II. Series.
  Z721.S66 2006
  027.009—dc22   2005024784

TABLE OF CONTENTS

INTRODUCTION

A TICKET TO THE WORLD

4

CHAPTER ONE

ANCIENT LIBRARIES

6

CHAPTER TWO

THE LIBRARY OF ALEXANDRIA AND OTHER EARLY LIBRARIES

11

CHAPTER THREE

THANK YOU, BEN FRANKLIN!

18

CHAPTER FOUR

OUR LIVING LIBRARY

23

CHAPTER FIVE

THE LIBRARY OF THE FUTURE

27

GLOSSARY

30

FOR FURTHER INFORMATION

31

INDEX

32

A TICKET TO THE WORLD

"**I**'m bored," Dan groaned. His brother Scott agreed. After three days of rain, who wouldn't be bored? Aunt Harriet decided everyone needed a change of scenery. She wrote two different lists of questions and gave one to each nephew.

"Come on," she said as she grabbed her car keys. "We're taking a trip around the world. Of course, we have to be home by 4:30." The boys thought Aunt Harriet was nuts. No one could travel around the world in three hours!

After driving for a few minutes, Aunt Harriet pulled into the library parking lot. "Whoa," said Scott. "This isn't a trip around the world—it's the library."

"You'll see," said Aunt Harriet. "You are going on a scavenger hunt through the library. The answers to these questions will take you around the world. The best part is you won't even have to leave the building."

The boys had to answer the following questions: What is the biggest desert in Asia? Where does the Orinoco River flow? Other questions asked about

Libraries offer resources that allow people to travel all over the world without actually leaving the building.

food, music, and sports. Scott and Dan combed through atlases, dictionaries, and a variety of nonfiction books. They used the library's computers and scanned the videos and books-on-tape. The answers they found took the boys to China, Russia, Canada, Scotland, and Brazil. What a trip!

That night at dinner, Uncle Buddy asked, "What did you guys do today?"

Dan and Scott grinned. "We went around the world."

CHAPTER ONE

ANCIENT LIBRARIES

Five thousand years ago, there were no books. The Sumerians, a culture that lived in present-day Iraq, wrote on clay tablets. They used a form of writing called **cuneiform. Scribes** prepared wet clay in molds. On that clay, they noted laws and wrote about schools, current events, tax payments, and court rulings. They also described religious rituals and created **hymns** and poetry. When the clay dried, it formed tablets. These tablets recorded life in a culture that disappeared centuries ago.

The Sumerians kept their tablets in storage rooms. The early libraries were places collecting recorded public information. Few people had personal libraries. There was no need for them. In those days, most people could not read or write.

Sumerians develop libraries to house clay tablets; Egyptians create libraries to store papyrus scrolls.

3000 B.C.

People in Egypt and Crete develop beeswax candles.

3000 B.C.: EGYPTIAN PAPYRUS

About the time the Sumerians were writing in clay, the Egyptians began using papyrus. Papyrus is a tall, reedy plant that grows beside the Nile River. Papyrus can be pounded into flat sheets, much like rough paper. The Egyptians wrote on the papyrus, then rolled their **documents** and tied them with string.

Early Egyptian scribes recorded the same information as the Sumerians—sales and taxes. They also wrote about warring **pharaohs.** They listed marriages, births, and deaths, too.

By 2400 B.C., an official in Egypt was named Scribe of the House of Books. This official acted as an early

DID YOU KNOW? ARCHAEOLOGISTS HAVE DUG UP MORE THAN 400,000 CLAY TABLETS IN WHAT USED TO BE MESOPOTAMIA (PRESENT-DAY IRAQ). MORE THAN 90 PERCENT OF THE TABLETS WERE IN COLLECTIONS—LIBRARIES—AND NOTED TAX PAYMENTS OR SALES OF GOODS OR PROPERTY.

Egyptians name an official Scribe of the House of Books (right).

2400 B.C.

Great Britain's Stonehenge is created.

librarian and safely stored the papyrus records that dealt with history and daily life in Egypt. Documents were sorted by topic. Wills, deeds, births, deaths, and marriages were stored in one section. Stories and poetry formed another section.

Unlike Sumerians, some wealthy Egyptians owned private libraries. They built rooms for storing scrolls in their homes. Archaeologists found one such library that dates back to 1635 B.C. and that contained more than 3,000 documents.

In the 600s B.C., Assyria (present-day Iraq) was at the height of its power. By that time, people had traveled and learned about other cultures. One such person was Ashurbanipal, king of Assyria.

1635 B.C.

A wealthy Egyptian owns a private library containing more than 3,000 documents.

In Southwest Asia, the Iron Age begins.

Ashurbanipal loved literature. He hoped to collect copies of all the stories, legends, and poems that had ever been created. By the time he died, Ashurbanipal owned a library with more than 25,000 texts containing writings about history, geography, science, and religion.

CA. 530 B.C.: GREEK PUBLIC LIBRARIES

The ancient Greeks developed a system for producing and distributing books. In about 530 B.C., libraries were places where people read and did research.

But not everyone respected the idea of libraries. King Xerxes of Persia invaded Greece in about 480 B.C. Xerxes burned Athens. The library and its books became piles of ashes.

Ashurbanipal (right) owns a library containing more than 25,000 volumes of literature.

600s B.C.

Assyria conquers Egypt.

Some historians claim that a Babylonian ruler named Seleucus rescued the library's contents. Others believe Seleucus destroyed all the books so that people would believe the world began with his rule.

If Seleucus *did* burn the books, he was not the only ruler to do so. In about 221 B.C., Emperor Shih Huang-ti ordered all the royal libraries in China burned. Books about farming and medicine were the only ones that were spared. But destroying books was not enough for Shih Huang-ti. He also ordered that anyone who knew the libraries' contents be burned alive. Under Shih Huang-ti, being a librarian was a dangerous job.

ca. 480 B.C.

Xerxes (left) burns the library of Athens.

Buddha dies.

CHAPTER TWO

THE LIBRARY OF ALEXANDRIA AND OTHER EARLY LIBRARIES

In the 300s B.C., a Greek commander named Alexander the Great spread his empire into Egypt. Ptolemy, one of Alexander's generals, became Egypt's governor after Alexander died in 323 B.C. But by 304 B.C., being governor was not enough for Ptolemy. He declared himself king. Ptolemy founded a great library in Alexandria, the city named to honor his former boss.

Ptolemy planned to have all the books in the world. According to legend, he sent letters to kings and rulers everywhere asking them to send copies of every document in their libraries. Books by Jewish **scholars,** Greek thinkers, and Arab mathematicians lined the walls of the library in Alexandria.

The books were sorted according to topic and source. Alexandria's

Ptolemy founds a library in Alexandria.

| ca. 290 B.C. |

Euclid (right) introduces ideas about geometry that spread throughout Greece.

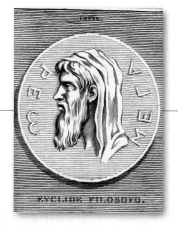

11

library may have been the greatest library of all time. Unfortunately, it was destroyed. The legends surrounding its destruction are almost as amazing as the library itself once was.

47 B.C.: FIRE!

In about 47 B.C., Roman commander Julius Caesar chased his enemy Pompey through Egypt. In a turnabout, Egyptian warships cut Caesar off from his military support on the Mediterranean. To save himself, Caesar sent his own ships to burn the

ca. 47 B.C.

According to one legend, Caesar burns Alexandria's library (left).

The New Year begins on January 1 for the first time.

Egyptian boats. According to one legend, the fire spread to the docks and buildings in Alexandria. The library caught fire. About 400,000 priceless documents burned to ashes.

Another legend of the library's destruction concerns a ruler in Alexandria named Theophilus. By A.D. 391, Alexandrians had become Christians. Theophilus believed he should stamp out all non-Christian temples. He burned the Temple of Serapis, which was next door to the library. As the temple burned, so did the buildings around it. The library destroyed in this fire had been built to replace the one Caesar had burned.

Religion also played a role in the next book burning involving the Alexandrian library. In about 640, the

According to another legend, Theophilus burns the library in Alexandria.

A.D. 391

Emperor Theodosius (right) declares Christianity to be the only acceptable religion.

13

Muslim leader Caliph Omar invaded Egypt. He ordered all books destroyed except those that followed the teachings of Mohammed, the main prophet of the Islamic religion. The library's scrolls were thrown on the fires that heated water for the local bathhouse. It took six months to burn them all.

Regardless of which legend is true—and perhaps all three are—the library of Alexandria disappeared.

CA. 730: PAPER AND PRINTING

Full credit goes to the Chinese for two remarkable inventions: paper and printing. The Chinese had been making writing paper since the second century A.D. Printing developed much later, in about 730. This involved char-

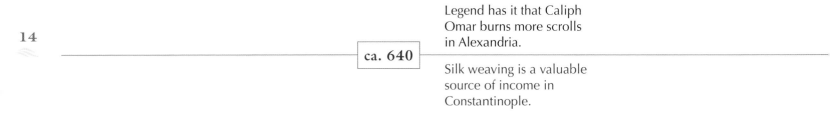

Legend has it that Caliph Omar burns more scrolls in Alexandria.

ca. 640

Silk weaving is a valuable source of income in Constantinople.

acters being carved onto wood blocks, smeared with ink, and pressed onto paper. The Chinese began making books, but it still took many years for this process to spread westward.

Papermaking took hold in the Arab world in about 750. Printing began there years later. Paper and printing eventually spread to Europe.

In Europe, making books was a slow process. The few people who could read and write were usually connected to the Roman Catholic Church. They were priests, monks, or nuns. Books were expensive and were limited to church libraries or wealthy individuals. Most books were handwritten and illustrated by monks. These books were

A SERIOUS CURSE AGAINST BOOK THIEVES
"FOR HIM THAT STEALETH A BOOK FROM THIS LIBRARY, LET IT CHANGE INTO A SERPENT IN HIS HAND AND REND HIM. LET HIM BE STRUCK WITH PALSY, AND ALL HIS MEMBERS BLASTED. LET HIM [SQUIRM] IN PAIN CRYING ALOUD FOR MERCY. . . . LET BOOKWORMS GNAW HIS ENTRAILS IN TOKEN OF THE WORM THAT DIETH NOT, AND WHEN AT LAST HE GOETH TO HIS FINAL PUNISHMENT, LET THE FLAMES OF HELL CONSUME HIM FOREVER."
—ATTRIBUTED TO THE MONASTERY OF SAN PEDRO, BARCELONA, SPAIN

ca. 730

The Chinese develop a simple process of printing.

Corn becomes a common crop raised by North American cultures.

called illuminated manuscripts, or "lighted" documents. Illuminated manuscripts were handwritten books painted with gold or silver ink. Decorated capital letters featured bright colors and were surrounded by different scenes. The added artwork "lightened" the book's text.

During the Middle Ages, European kings, princes, and other nobles sometimes kept private libraries in their castles. Churches also had libraries for priests, nuns, rabbis, and other religious leaders. As the Roman Catholic Church built universities, it built libraries in those schools. Some early libraries still exist at European universities such as Oxford,

Monks illustrate the *Book of Kells* (left).

ca. 800

Charlemagne is crowned the First Holy Roman Emperor.

Cambridge, and the Sorbonne.

It might seem that Johannes Gutenberg's movable type printing press, which was invented in the mid-1400s, would have made books cheaper. It did bring down cost a little. But consider this: Nicolaus Copernicus's book about the Earth revolving around the Sun was printed in 1543. The book cost about $200 in today's money. At that time, a European worker earned less than $100 per year. Few people could afford to buy even one book in a lifetime. Besides, most people couldn't read. What would they do with a book?

Johannes Gutenberg develops the movable-type printing press (right).

The Aztec Empire begins in Central America.

CHAPTER THREE

THANK YOU, BEN FRANKLIN!

B y the early 1700s, education became more common, and so did books. Most people learned to read. Families sat in their parlors and read passages from the Bible or printed sermons. But while colleges, churches, and the wealthy had libraries, public libraries did not yet exist in America's colonies.

Inventor and politician Benjamin Franklin decided to try an experiment in Philadelphia, Pennsylvania. In 1731, Franklin founded a lending library called the Library Company of Philadelphia. Readers joined the **subscription** library and rented books, just as you might rent a movie from a video store.

By 1769, several independent libraries—including Franklin's—formed one library group. Franklin's subscription library eventually developed into the Philadelphia Public Library, the first American library open to the public. Other

Benjamin Franklin founds the Library Company of Philadelphia.

1731

The first concert in the colonies is held in Boston.

Philadelphia's subscription libraries join to form one central library.

1769

Future French emperor Napoléon Bonaparte is born.

colonial cities supported the idea of public libraries. Most of those libraries, like Ben Franklin's library, offered pay-as-you-read books.

1800: THE LIBRARY OF CONGRESS

Before he became U.S. president, James Madison served as a Virginia congressman and suggested the construction of a national library. Other congressmen agreed. In 1800, the Library of Congress was formed. The early library was not the giant project it is today. By 1802, the Library of Congress had a whopping 964 books and 9 maps or charts.

During the War of 1812 (1812–1814), the British set fire to the U.S. Capitol. The fire destroyed most of the

1800

The Library of Congress (right) is founded.

The U.S. Congress meets in Washington, D.C., for the first time.

19

Library of Congress, which was housed in the Capitol. Fortunately, former president Thomas Jefferson had a huge private library. He also was quite wealthy. He agreed to sell his personal library to Congress for $23,950. Horse-drawn carts carried Jefferson's 6,487 books to the temporary library at Blodgett's Hotel in Washington, D.C.

1876: A BIG YEAR FOR LIBRARIES

Free public libraries became common throughout Europe and most American countries during the 1800s. In the United States, the town of Peterborough, New Hampshire, opened the first tax-supported library in 1833. Citizens paid taxes on their earnings or their property to a city or state. Some of that money was then used to buy

1833

Peterborough, New Hampshire, opens a tax-funded public library.

The American Anti-Slavery Society is founded (left).

books for libraries and pay for a librarian. Boston's public library was founded in 1848.

Major improvements on public libraries came in 1876. First, the American Library Association (ALA) was founded. To this day, the ALA is the major national organization for librarians. In 1876, the first publication of the *Library Journal* was closely tied to the founding of the ALA. The *Library Journal* reviews books and offers suggestions on library practices and services.

The final important event in 1876 occurred when a young man named Melvil Dewey introduced a system for classifying books. In the Dewey Decimal Classification (DDC) system, every topic has a number that can be placed

Melvil Dewey (right) creates the DDC system, the ALA is founded, and the *Library Journal* is first published.

1876

Alexander Graham Bell receives a patent for the telephone.

21

in a catalog. For example, 973.7 points to books on the Civil War (1861–1865). Snakes fall under 597.96. This system continues to play an important role in modern-day libraries.

Public library systems experienced tremendous growth during the 1900s. Libraries offered more services. In 1905, the first horse-drawn bookmobile carted books through the streets of Hagerstown, Maryland. During the 1900s, wealthy businessman Andrew Carnegie built hundreds of public libraries using his own money. During the Great Depression (1929–1939), the Works Progress Administration (WPA) put out-of-work men back on the job—building libraries. Carnegie and WPA libraries continue to provide services in hundreds of communities.

1905

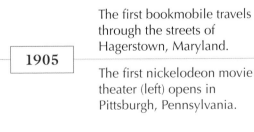

The first bookmobile travels through the streets of Hagerstown, Maryland.

The first nickelodeon movie theater (left) opens in Pittsburgh, Pennsylvania.

CHAPTER FOUR

OUR LIVING LIBRARY

The Library of Congress is the largest library in the United States. **Patrons** can find Lincoln's Gettysburg Address, written in Lincoln's handwriting. Or they can read one of the drafts of the Declaration of Independence, as written by Jefferson. Most importantly, the Library of Congress is open to everyone.

Books come in all sizes, and the Library of Congress has some unusual volumes. The library's smallest book is *Old King Cole*. It is .04 inches (1.02 millimeters) by .04 inches (1.02 mm), and its pages are turned with a needle. The largest book is *Birds of America* by John James Audubon, measuring 39.37 inches (1 meter) high.

The Library of Congress has developed special collections that deal

1912

The *Titanic* sinks off the
coast of Newfoundland.

> "THROUGHOUT MY FORMAL
> EDUCATION I SPENT MANY, MANY
> HOURS IN PUBLIC AND SCHOOL
> LIBRARIES. . . . THE CURRENT
> DEFINITIVE ANSWER TO ALMOST
> ANY QUESTION CAN BE FOUND
> WITHIN THE FOUR WALLS OF
> MOST LIBRARIES."
> —ARTHUR ASHE,
>   TENNIS CHAMPION

with art, history, culture, and science. One of the library's earliest divisions was the Asian collection. It began with 933 volumes donated by the emperor of China. Today, the Asian division houses 2 million books, magazines, pieces of art, and manuscripts from all over Asia. Works in Chinese, Japanese, Korean, and a variety of Southeast Asian languages are contained in the Asian collection.

In 1914, the library opened its Hebraic section. This quickly became one of the largest collections of Jewish religious and historic texts. The collection is written in either Hebrew or Yiddish, a German language that uses Hebrew characters.

1914

The Library of Congress adds a Hebraic section.

World War I (1914–1918) begins in Europe.

1931: BOOKS IN BRAILLE

In 1931, the Library of Congress began producing books in **braille** for blind readers. This led to recorded books. Blind library patrons throughout the United States could hear the Declaration of Independence, Shakespeare's plays, or Emily Dickinson's poetry read aloud. All types of printed materials are recorded daily. Today, the Library of Congress's "talking book" library distributes 22 million recorded and braille titles to more than 760,000 blind readers yearly.

The library constantly adds new collections. In

1931

The Library of Congress begins producing books in braille (right).

The United States is caught in the Great Depression.

1954

The Near East collection offers newspapers, magazines, books, art, and rare documents from all over the Arab world.

The U.S. Supreme Court rules against segregation in schools.

1954, the Near East collection was formed. This collection includes newspapers, magazines, books, art, and rare documents from all over the Arab world. Thirty-eight languages are represented in the Near East collection.

In 1976, the library added the American Folklife Center to preserve and present American folk history. This is a truly unique collection, offering sound recordings, manuscripts, oral histories, Native American music, and photographs.

Today's Library of Congress houses nearly 130 million books, journals, newspapers, maps, letters, diaries, works of art, speeches, records, movies, and photos. It preserves the history of our nation and the culture of the world.

The American Folklife Center opens at the Library of Congress.

1976

Cray-1 (left), the first commercially available supercomputer, is developed.

CHAPTER FIVE

THE LIBRARY OF THE FUTURE

Libraries are living, changing, growing things. They open windows to history and science. They become doors to the imagination. Libraries change to meet the needs of their patrons. The future of libraries lies not in buildings, but in services. One of the greatest of these services is making the library's materials available through the Internet.

Patrons can access some of the Library of Congress's contents by visiting its Web site. In 1989, the American Memory project opened a gateway to American history and culture. The project is a **digital** collection that features more than 10 million items, including newspapers, books, oral histories, songs, and photos. All of these items are accessible on the Internet.

Virtual libraries—libraries on the Internet—have become common. In

The American Memory project
begins at the Library of Congress.

1989

The Berlin Wall is torn down.

> "A GREAT LIBRARY CONTAINS THE DIARY OF THE HUMAN RACE."
> —GEORGE MERCER DAWSON, EXPLORER

1994, the World Wide Web Virtual Library opened for business. A year later, the Internet Public Library project at the University of Michigan got its start. Today, an Internet search of "virtual library" reveals millions of hits. Online libraries take you on museum tours. They allow you to enter chemistry labs, hospitals, and art studios.

One such online library is the International Children's Digital Library (ICDL), a project of the University of Maryland and the Internet Archive. The ICDL is a public library designed for children from ages three to thirteen. The project hopes to collect more than 10,000 books in at least 100 languages. All materials are free to children, teachers, librarians, and parents around the world.

1994

The World Wide Web Virtual Library opens for business on the Internet.

Nelson Mandela is elected president of South Africa.

1995

The Internet Public Library gets its start.

Eileen Collins becomes the first woman to pilot a space shuttle mission aboard the *Discovery*.

To go to tomorrow's library, you
will never have to leave your room. Harry
Potter, the Velveteen Rabbit, and a host of
other characters will step through cyber-
space and into your computer. Libraries
will offer films, magazines, plays, and
poetry with ready access. You will tour the
world's greatest libraries with the click of a
mouse.

Fortunately, nothing will ever replace
story time. A hundred years from now, a
librarian will still open young minds with
four simple words: *Once upon a time* . . . .

The Library of Congress commits
to making all of its collections
available to people doing online
research (right).

1996

Bill Clinton defeats Bob
Dole in the U.S. presidential
election.

braille (BRAYL)
Braille is a system of raised dots that allows blind people to read by touch. The Library of Congress offers a wide range of braille books.

cuneiform (kyoo-NEE-uh-form)
Cuneiform is a form of writing that features wedge-shaped characters. Sumerians used cuneiform to record tax payments.

digital (DIJ-uh-tuhl)
Digital electronics use numbers to record images or text so that they can later be accessed on a computer. The Library of Congress's American Memory project is a digital collection that features newspapers, books, oral histories, songs, and photos.

documents (DOK-yuh-muhntz)
Documents are pieces of written material. The Egyptians saved documents recording births, marriages, and deaths.

hymns (HIMZ)
Hymns are songs that are often sung in religious ceremonies. Sumerian scribes recorded hymns on clay tablets.

manuscripts (MAN-yuh-skriptz)
Manuscripts are written materials, such as books, plays, poems, or letters. During the Middle Ages, monks illustrated manuscripts with beautiful designs.

patrons (PAY-truhnz)
Patrons are people who regularly use the services of a certain business. The Library of Congress offers a wide collection of braille and recorded books to its blind patrons.

pharaohs (FAIR-ohz)
Pharaohs were rulers in ancient Egypt. Egyptian scribes wrote about warring pharaohs.

scholars (SKOL-urz)
Scholars are people who have studied one or more topics and who are therefore extremely knowledgeable about certain subjects. Books written by great scholars filled Alexandria's library.

scribes (SKRYBZ)
Scribes were people who could write in ancient times. Sumerian scribes wrote on clay tablets.

subscription (suhb-SKRIP-shuhn)
A subscription is a paid membership in a group. Philadelphia's colonists joined subscription libraries.

FOR FURTHER INFORMATION

AT THE LIBRARY

Nonfiction

Appelt, Kathi, and Jeanne Cannella Schmitzer.
*Down Cut Shin Creek: The Pack Horse Librarians of
Kentucky.* New York: HarperCollins, 2001.

* Bisbort, Alan, and Linda Barret Osborne.
*The Nation's Library: The Library of Congress,
Washington, D.C.* Washington, D.C.: The Library of
Congress, 2000.

Simon, Charnan. *Andrew Carnegie: Builder of
Libraries.* Danbury, Conn.: Children's Press, 1997.

* Trumble, Kelly, and Robina MacIntyre Marshall
(illustrator). *The Library of Alexandria.* New York:
Clarion Books, 2003.

Waxman, Sydell, Patty Gallinger (illustrator), and Liz
Milkau (illustrator). *Believing in Books: The Story of
Lillian Smith.* Toronto: Napoleon Publishing, 2002.

Fiction

Clifford, Eth, and George Hughes (illustrator). *Help!
I'm a Prisoner in the Library.* Boston: Houghton
Mifflin, 1979.

*Books marked with a star are challenge reading material
for those reading above grade level.*

ON THE WEB

Visit our home page for lots of links about libraries:
http://www.childsworld.com/links

Note to Parents, Teachers, and Librarians:
We routinely check our Web links to make sure they're
safe, active sites—so encourage your readers to check
them out!

PLACES TO VISIT OR CONTACT

American Library Association
50 East Huron
Chicago, IL 60611
800/545-2433

Library of Congress
1st Street and East Capitol Street SE
Washington, DC 20540
202/707-5000

Your Local Public Library
Be sure to get your own library card!

INDEX

Alexander the Great, 11
Alexandria, Egypt, 11–12, 13, 14
American Folklife Center, 26
American Library Association (ALA), 21
American Memory project, 27
Ashurbanipal, king of Assyria, 8–9
Asian collection (Library of Congress), 24
Assyria, 8
atlases, 5
Audubon, John James, 23

Bibliotheca Alexandria, 14
Blodgett's Hotel, 20
Book of Kells (illuminated manuscript), 16
bookmobiles, 22
books-on-tape, 5, 25
braille, 25

Caesar, Julius, 12–13
Carnegie, Andrew, 22
China, 14, 24

clay tablets, 6, 7
computers, 5, 29
Copernicus, Nicolaus, 17
cuneiform writing, 6

Declaration of Independence, 23, 25
Dewey Decimal Classification (DDC) system, 21–22
Dewey, Melvil, 21
dictionaries, 5

Egypt, 7–8, 11–14

Franklin, Benjamin, 18, 19

Gettysburg Address, 23
Great Depression, 22
Greece, 9–10, 11
Gutenberg, Johannes, 17
Hebraic section (Library of Congress), 24

illuminated manuscripts, 16

International Children's Digital Library (ICDL), 28
Internet, 27–29
Internet Public Library project, 28

Jefferson, Thomas, 20, 23

Library Company of Philadelphia, 18
Library Journal, 21
Library of Congress, 19–20, 23–24, 25–26, 27

Madison, James, 19

Mesopotamia, 7
Mohammed (Islamic prophet), 14
Monastery of San Pedro, 15
movable type printing press, 17

Near East collection (Library of Congress), 26
nonfiction books, 5

Omar (Muslim leader), 14

paper, 14, 15
papyrus, 7, 8
Philadelphia Public Library, 18
Plutarch (Greek writer), 13
printing, 14–15, 17
Ptolemy, king of Egypt, 11

Roman Catholic Church, 15, 16

Scribe of the House of Books, 7–8
scribes, 6, 7–8
Seleucus (Babylonian ruler), 10
Shih Huang-ti (emperor of China), 10
Sumeria, 6

"talking books," 25
taxes, 20–21
Temple of Serapis, 13
Theophilus (Egyptian ruler), 13

University of Maryland, 28
University of Michigan, 28

videos, 5
virtual libraries, 27–29

War of 1812, 19
World Wide Web Virtual Library, 28

Xerxes, king of Persia, 9

ABOUT THE AUTHOR

BARBARA SOMERVILL IS THE AUTHOR OF MANY BOOKS FOR CHILDREN. SHE LOVES LEARNING AND SEES EVERY WRITING PROJECT AS A CHANCE TO LEARN NEW INFORMATION OR GAIN A NEW UNDERSTANDING. MS. SOMERVILL GREW UP IN NEW YORK STATE, BUT HAS ALSO LIVED IN TORONTO, CANADA; CANBERRA, AUSTRALIA; CALIFORNIA; AND SOUTH CAROLINA. SHE CURRENTLY LIVES WITH HER HUSBAND IN SIMPSONVILLE, SOUTH CAROLINA.